THE HAUNTING

CATE PEEBLES

PRIOR WINNERS OF THE
TUPELO PRESS SNOWBOUND CHAPBOOK AWARD

Emma Binder, *Country Songs for Alice* — Selected by Hala Alyan

Matthew Gellman, *Night Logic* — Selected by Denise Duhamel

Eric Pankey, *The Future Perfect* — Selected by John Yau

Tyler Mills, *City Scattered* — Selected by Cole Swenson

Chad Bennett, *Artifact of a Bygone Era* — Selected by Eduardo C. Corral

Meg Wade, *Slick Like Dark* — Selected by Kristina Marie Darling

Matt Donovan, *Rapture & the Big Bam* — Selected by Lia Purpura

Allan Peterson, *Other Than They Seem* — Selected by Ruth Ellen Kocher

Chad Parmenter, *Weston's Unsent Letters to Modotti* — Selected by Kathleen Jesme

Deborah Flanagan, *Or, Gone* — Selected by Christopher Buckley

Anna George Meek, *Engraved* — Selected by Ellen Doré Watson

Kathleen Jesme, *Meridian* — Selected by Patricia Fargnoli

Brandon Som, *Babel's Moon* — Selected by Aimee Nezhukumatathil

Stacey Waite, *the lake has no saint* — Selected by Dana Levin

John Cross, *staring at the animal* — Selected by Gillian Conoley

Cecilia Woloch, *Narcissus* — Selected by Marie Howe

Joy Katz, *The Garden Room* — Selected by Lisa Russ Spaar

Mark Yakich, *The Making of Collateral Beauty* — Selected by Mary Ruefle

David Hernandez, *A House Waiting for Music* — Selected by Ray Gonzalez

Barbara Tran, *In the Mynah Bird's Own Words* — Selected by Robert Wrigley

WINNER OF THE SNOWBOUND CHAPBOOK AWARD

Cate Peebles is author of *Thicket* (Lost Roads Press, 2018), as well as five chapbooks, including *Sun King*, winner of the 2024 Tomaž Šalamun Prize Editors' Choice Selection from Factory Hollow Press and *The Woodlands* (Sixth Finch Books, 2016). Her work has appeared in numerous print and online magazines, such as *The American Poetry Review*, *Bayou*, *Bennington Review*, *DIAGRAM*, *diode*, *Ploughshares*, and *Volt*. A coeditor of the occasional online poetry magazine, *Fou*, she is an archivist and lives in Pittsburgh, PA.

The Haunting is the full-length expansion of Cate Peebles' prize-winning chapbook selection entitled *Revenge Bodies*.

RECENT AND SELECTED TITLES FROM TUPELO PRESS

THE HAUNTING

CATE PEEBLES

TUPELO PRESS
NORTH ADAMS, MA

The Haunting
Copyright © 2025 Cate Peebles. All rights reserved.

ISBN-13: 978-1-961209-22-0 (paper)
Library of Congress Control Number: 2024038166

Design by Allison O'Keefe

First paperback edition January 2025

Tupelo Press
P.O. Box 1767
North Adams, Massachusetts 01247
(413) 664-9611 / Fax: (413) 664-9711
editor@tupelopress.org / www.tupelopress.org

Tupelo Press is an award-winning independent literary press that publishes fine fiction, non-fiction, and poetry in books that are a joy to hold as well as read. Tupelo Press is a registered 501(c)(3) non-profit organization, and we rely on public support to carry out our mission of publishing extraordinary work that may be outside the realm of the large commercial publishers. Financial donations are welcome and are tax deductible.

for my mother and our mothers and our mothers' mothers

She herself is a haunted house. She does not possess herself; her ancestors sometimes come and peer out of the windows of her eyes and that is very frightening.

Angela Carter, "The Lady of the House of Love"

My knives are like a tongue—

Louise Bourgeois

Contents

Note Stitched Above the Monster's Eye

Oh, praise - - - my rage - - - - - - - - - - - - - - - - -

Abstract

I feel I am reborn blazing/ dead hounds/ baying from beyond/ if memory serves/ each calls the hour when a haunt passes by/ in a hunt/ you know/ they're not dogs/ they're hounds and they don't bark/ they bay/ such sounds I've made when loosening the chains of knowledge/ glistening/ the horses stabled/ their haunches secured in ink/ I become totally obsessed with down-to-earth catastrophes/ the mayor in a ditch/ the parson upside-down/ tossed from a cantering stallion he'd just met/ I rode my horse through a flash flood/ her coat/ lightning fresh/ electricity shatters a pastoral sky/ befits neural pathways of a bright woman racing/ apace with sunset/ the evening blisters/ a red crystal cup filled with broken crystal stags/ Dad tended the fire/ Mom slept in an ice tub/ the rest of the party was drawing pictures of sweet vendettas/ with hot charcoal and vitriol/ down by the raging creek/ we had come to a point that had no home/ beyond rippled sinew/ I knew things and sensed what I didn't/ limbs akimbo are/ my idea of lights out/ horses sleep standing/ I sleep when I fly/ at the gong of midnight/ hounds announce/ the bridal party exiting the elevator/ but my fox mask and riding silks throw them/ their gowns/ pool in gutters/ the gowns/ the gowns/ hanging red/ exquisite as bloodbaths/ it is not my wedding day/ but the hunt belongs to me—

The Worm

Worms be your words, you not safe from ours

John Ashbery, "Sonnet"

The worm was the
first thing on earth;
splitting its body into
endless godheads in a
field of bursting
milkweed pods.

It lived in the garden,
a plurality longing to
be a snake, but shrank
in beige desert light.

The worm is a blip. A
blot. A blood hungry
haunt in love with
harrowing.

Eyeless flicker of an
umbilical tube,
wriggling cuticles
electric waves
crowding out the sea.

Ringing so through
time—a flooded mud
hole. It gets by just
fine without a heart—

The American Way of Death I

The green porch swing/ dangles directly in the sun/ our sickly ash cut down/ the roof has a different face/ now/ freckled rafters/ I am/ the haunt/ and the house awaiting diagnosis/ unfit to exist/ under conditions of abject/ reality my beauty/ routine equals 15 lotions/ carnival masks for/ 71 potential squamous/ cells/ I've inherited this predisposition/ to catching on fire/ sizzler/ exit 28/ highway 59/ there is a fear in me/ a sensitivity to substance and substances/ running down the road in a blackout/ I will vomit on your wall/ possessed by a coal miner's black lung/ limp canary in a brass cage/ on the floor/ I went too far down/ and I will make you carry me home/ and blame my ancestors for everything/ I don't like about myself/ this is my good side/ so whatever death/ I'm given/ will suit the narrative/ still/ so scary/ sometimes inheritance cracked open/ is an empty chest/ I moved to the Deep South/ to recon/ with an inability to recon with/ history/ made a mess/ of it/ the grandmothers say/ get out/ you don't belong/ where you came from/ after all/ these infinite mothers/ sitting out front on a single swing/ swaddled in vinegar poultices/ for the fever/ all their bodies/ one blue flame/ they say go away/ but it was a nice/ idea/ at the time/ sweet tea/ humidity curls/ crown this temple/ they made me/ a wet face/ that's barely mine

Bingo of Brides Stripped Bare

Cracked glass in transit—	Silver dress grown lonely in a drawer of stained satin scarves—	Lace lacks secrecy, a looky-loo's knotted shroud—
Crepe roses wilted to match hums loose in a marble atrium—	An old phone slams into its orange moon cradle—	Whose trashed azaleas, tiger lilies, and rosy phlox dampen under dew at the dump today—
Your aorta got shorted—	Delete conversation	Empty guest book cellophane veils blank memory ovals and lines—
A maiden name makes molten gold daggers—	New blue vow borrows old crystal to smash with a satin-wrapped hymnal—	A mountainous vista slips through fingers and stains a silk slip—
Don't give me away but a way to get even—	Hand wash only with lithe witty scythes—	—in bowls of ice and blood

Note Stitched Inside the Monster's Mouth

It was   already   night - - - in   the
heavens - - - when   I   considered   what
had passed - - - I hid myself in - - - - -

- - cold stars - - - against - - - the fever
of my blood - - - and - - - crept into -
- - - thick underwood - - - - - - - - - -

visited by - - - my hunger - - - however
- - - I knew - - - and waited - - - to
discover - - - the meaning - - - - - - -

~

You sip tea from a paper cup. Bergamot milk-sweat still wet above your lip.

It started again with a wish, a tickle in the ear. The worm was hungry. The worm wanted a new home. You had an empty tunnel glowing that the worm could taste, could fill. What a privilege to let it lodge. It burrows across the earth for you. A gift and a grift.

The worm's tail lives in another woman's body. Its head pokes into the shell-curve of your cochlea finding a vibration you like. It's a thin string, a braid around your crown meandering to the rib cage—

atria and ventricles, its favorite mouthful.

The Alphabet

Mother/ didn't teach me about bleeding/ she pointed to a shelf/ and I learned to swaddle myself/ the sun/ stuttered down the blinds/ and stains began to set/ she recited/ the catechism in her head/ backwards/ in bed/ her legs up the wall/ to improve blood flow/ to the amygdala/ crisscrossed her lips/ with green light/ yellow twine/ I asked her/ what're you saying/ but she showed me/ the definition of dynamite/ opened her soundless mouth/ speech is explosion/ pointed with one finger/ your birth/ pitched to death/ rigid vein-wrapped femur / it learns to let go/ a stag's antlers shedding in December/ repeats renewal/ mimics branches/ how did you pick my name?/ I once asked/ She closed my eyes/ finger to lip/ shh/ pointed to an empty page/ catharsis/ I could have been something/ she saw/ and plucked/ from the garden/ I write new endings on blank pages/ after the afterward/ as a kid/ I made jelly sandwiches/ to eat in a dark closet/ a rocket cockpit/ reading Jane Eyre/ rehearsed her ire/ red rooms in every cell/ I drew a horse/ scribbled mad/ blue fingers/ in a thatched basket/ wondered/ what could be/ scarier than birth/ an ordinary terror/ it's nothing/ personal/ so

Kwaidan

A woman returns/ to the home where she died/ a switchblade in every pocket/ a silver shade/ nesting with sparrows/ in the attic/ where the family knives are stored/ blades/ effortlessly upfront/ about what they do best/ not mastering a craft/ but crafting paper masks/ take/ a walk/ with me/ she says/ she/ hovers in a rafter/ walk/ through a thresher/ remembering the uncut/ days/ but shredded/ gravel/ good as emeralds/ swinging/ bottle green/ drape her sword-threaded clavicle/ the pointed rush/ a yellow slip hangs/ over a screen/ husband/ you chose another/ so she comes back/ all edges/ a sharp fog/ woman/ rain painted thick/ against the window/ she watches with/ her fingertips/ dragged through/ ragged mist/ flays it/ with a touch/ the groan/ a white robe/ indigo fringe/ hands & arms/ made of glass/ & steel/ visceral daggers/ cleave her widowed parts/ gutted eyes/ lungs/ spleen/ heart/ dangles/ black hair/ bandages thread wind/ she waits for him/ behind a door/ floating razorblades/ redder/ than exile/ in a s/well of/ frayed ribbon & bone

~

The worm fills the first woman's mouth with caked muck as it exits. It drags a trail from her tongue across the carpet, the porch, the highway, the sky, as it writhes away.

The worm mines you. Consumes interior offal and firmament as you sleep.

The worm curls around your foot hanging off the bed, awake all night, the longest tongue. It says nothing but sludge with illegible script written into your skin; through your sheets a sweaty terror twists the way water barely spills from a spinning bucket.

The worm fits your shape with its skin.

Tattooed blue magnolia, dead stars, catfish whiskers and a faded map of the Ozarks. Every corner it says yes to, agrees with, every door in your nervous system it opens. It waits for you to go first. *After you.*

It follows.

Wuthering Heights, Volume I

I have just returned

to unchain it

a short history of

desire

the earth was hard

I grasped the latch and

                                         seized

                                         radiance

She looked at me
                    motionless
                    afraid

                    ghosts

            among us

    snow

        —all 'round

close at my ear   warm
          blood

                              in the dark

                    the earth
          through every limb

                              refilled the grave
                              with

          breath

Horror Movie Bingo

A fresh start in the country is all she needs—	City life, an ambulance ringing red through her head—	The way light catches under a closet door—
Amulets, handprints, stains—	Mirror propped to catch you in the window covered in mauve gauze—	She runs down basement stairs into the darker dark where there's nothing but walls—
Whose eyes in the glass? Whose hand in the water? Whose red hair spread on stone?	Is anybody there?	Gold eyes glow gold— eyes glow gold all night— a tentacle embrace—
The future was born yesterday— holding an invisible hand, cold in the dark—	A mad, bad woman whose lust is a tabernacle spooled in a box tucked under floorboards—	Two children whistling in the empty playground—
Hello?	The answer is always a séance or an archive—	The end is never ending—

Note Stitched Across the Monster's Cheek

Icy - - and glittering peaks - - I
was troubled by - - traces of - -
winter avalanche - - and whose
death - - looking at stars - - the
laughter died away - - hoping
some change - - would take
place - - I quitted the scene - -
the world before me - - a hell
within - - the cottage was dark -
- dark - - pines rose - - borne
away by waves - - the sea room
- - was frozen - - hard - - and
chill - - and bare - - I wandered
- - wide - - from there - - - - - - -

Carnival of Souls

Me and my/ roadster sped/ off the bridge right/ into the river/ it was like I died/ and the world/ had washed by/ cleansing itself of/ my permission/ and I'm dripping on the shore/ climbing up a slope/ onto the dusty road/ to catch a ride to town/ an organ plays under my fingers/ neither cold nor warm/ bone light/ take me away to the desert/ or just near/ where it begins/ that edge/ is my shelter/ I'll start again/ no one will know what/ an end it was/ because I return slash emerge with/ a suitcase full/ of crisp/ sheet music/ while everything moves/ around me/ it's hard to describe/ the lament/ it's that/ when I am lost/ no one will look at me/ look/ for me/ among the dancing/ dead/ on the platform/ we shared/ stalled trains/ an exchange/ one car into another/ I run/ without a reflection/ in the window/ reaching into the sky/ the trees are so many/ women/ still celestial bodies/ astral/ really/ bowing up to the sun/ so much unseen/ the organ plays on/ devotionals/ behind my back/ this ghost/ I can feel her/ glittering/ past my sleeves

Psycho

I've been called/ worse surely/ the road erased/ by a shower/ so thick it thinks/ it's a string section/ roughly bowed/ by horsehair dragged on catgut/ the screech and stutter/ of sheets beating/ windshield or wings/ stuffed ravens/ placed in every corner/ of the sky/ the sound on the other end of a receiver/ hello?/ nothing/ hello?/ then tears/ a full cup spilled/ into the gap before news/ is said/ in gasps/ everyone running/ away from something/ it would seem/ a fix-all for every problem/ the drive inside the drive/ manifested in messy/ vision and pulling over/ to wait out the storm/ at a roadside motel/ 10,000 dollars/ hiding in the back seat/ leaves me/ feeling so unclean/ needing steam/ a shower hot enough/ to last/ past the end credits/ eyes forever/ open/ to the light/ that came at last/ the fogged curtain covered/ in dripping beads/ violins play familiar/ unravel/ a sense of/ she/ no I/ should know better/ this time/ heartstops/ a body bent/ toward what it lacks/ thumped heavy/ into cold/ white tiles

Psycho II

A woman on the road/ alone at night/ should know this/ or that knife trick/ how/ to hold her thumb/ just so/ to land/ a punch how to/ fold herself weaponlike/ against a wall/ her skin divining obscurity/ and how to/ drive faster/ a quick/ left before/ dozing off a cliff/ isn't destiny/ funny that way/ it gets so shrill it swells/ your tongue/ she means well/ she might/ but is she a/ wrong one/ is she/ escaping some/ son/ look this was all supposed to go/ so differently/ but men creep in/ canonically they tell you again/ how to protect yourself/ against them/ the motel sheets folded/ and clean the door/ shuts tidy with a click/ but night bleeds through/ and smells like cheap soap/ foaming in her hand/ she stands in a stream/ hot mascara a nighthawk/ on her cheek the dark/ comes down familiar/ as it falls across/ cream curtains pulled/ ice melting in a glass/ of spirits/ her gaze full and wide/ it opens a ring/ of stars that are/ her teeth/ the wind is screaming/ something about discretion/ naked lamplight/ in fog/ doesn't reveal a thing

Carrie

Away from the gymnasium/ red balloons crowd the corners/ of my
eyes/ all the kids lit up silvery/ how mean they are how/ cruel the
kindest/ can be/ taunts smiling with their hands/ held open in the fire/
see how they flee/ see them laugh at me/ daisy petal teeth/ rotten with
chewing gum/ firecracker ash/ just give me a minute/ to calm my/
knives in dirt/ reach my arms into the earth/ I forgot grace/ forgot
memory/ forgot the veil/ big enough to cover our burning mouths/ a
youthful glow gone pyrotechnic/ when I let my soul/ be known/ it wore
a pink gown/ it said dance/ with me/ please and he took me/ close to
his warm skin/ drew me a poem/ in Astroturf/ pinched green against
my cheek/ and cut open the heavy white/ roses cinched around my wrist

Prom Night

Trails of/ glitter tracked inside my
walls/ I'll never be rid/ of the pink and
gold flecks/ stuck to my shoes/ my
heart/ my hair/ with sweat/ a
glistening/ I've followed everywhere/
there is nothing/ I want/ to let myself
love/ more than/ dancing and falling/
so far/ into a song's wound/ a glowing
grave all tangled with words/ so I ask/
the dancefloor/ to swallow me/ whole

~

The worm slurps
your intestines and
muscles its way
toward an exit.
Gutted. Again, the
heat of another body
pulls it out, a
hungering thread
binding you shut on
its way to her, her
warm breasts filled
for feeding, mouth
open like a flattened
orchid.

The worm is an
obvious creature. It
does not know itself,
repeats
itself
endlessly,
automatically,
cylindrically.
Seeking succor.

It hums *Lay, Lady,
Lay* anxious to suckle
her grief. Still twisting
on your tongue as it
licks her tears, finds
her nostril, hangs like
a bridge between as it
has done since before
the first garden
burned.

A ding in your neck as
its tail flicks your
cheek, a bell, your
body retching peals.

Gaslight

Even wisdom's a bandaged ambassador/ her cheeks
mashed pulpy/ errant plum skin in ice wine/ the blood of
saints sold as a tincture/ for hysteria spilled/ in your
messenger bag/ soaks right through the sheet music for a
song about blackouts/ I never met a piece of advice I
followed/ into the sunset/ only strangers/ girl/ girl/ girl/
he's been upstairs dimming the lights/ this whole time/
and you knew it/ but it's in my head how Chopin sounds
great/ living or dead/ and a corsage of damp azalais/ at
my breast/ don't stop singing/ I haven't left the attic in
months/ but will do better in the next life/ I recognize a
rut/ Lo!/ let's all do exquisitely disastrous things!/
strawberry ice cream calls from the freezer/ you can tell a
girl not to get bangs/ but why try/ the bags are packed
and I'm moving to Mississippi/ damn knowing/ Reader/
I jumped in his rusty pickup-truck anyway/ even though
all he wanted was to steal the rubies/ hidden in my hair/
my most secret beauties/ traded for their weight in
widows/ I'll be the biggest fool ever/ running as fast as I
can/ scissors raised/ blades pointed straight/ through the
aurora borealis/ piercing the north star's nebulous womb

Leave Her to Heaven

Eternity is the exact/
shade of lime/ as my seat
cushion/ the same
amount of time/ it will
take/ to sit in this clinic/
and listen to Nothing/
Compares 2 U/ in its
entirety/ as a nurse
draws blood/ from a
faint vein/ she flicks at
its/ shying/ the needle
pressed into/ a bruise/
finding only unpolished
marble/ think of the
time you hurt/ most and
how it gave birth to you/
a sequel/ test results
indicate/ there's more to
the story/ because the
end/ of a story/ is only a
fallen body before it
rises/ again/ the room
was/ a rectory/
miracles/ sting me/ I
bleed/ like a stone saint

The Heiress

Mothers and fathers/ of the world/ who am I/ allowed to be/ now what is my blood/ for and what happens/ to my love/ when cashed in for mud/ masks that remove/ impurities/ from deep within/ what am I/ now when I am nobody/ 's mother and my body is all/ mine/ its gold and coal/ burns for nights on end/ or gets spent at the corner store/ on sour miniature lemons/ that fill my empty/ palm and stick between my crowns/ what can I say/ about my womb/ it is made of multiplied colossal/ cities in which I thought I knew/ other people and myself/ how we lived/ echoed and wrecked under overgrown virgin/ forests/ sequoia cypress hemlock fir/ growing over crushed skyscrapers/ unpeopled shopping centers/ powdered parking lots now lush with fronds and needles/ red leaves hiding/ nests surrounded by broken/ blue eggshells/ all birds and the negatives of birds/ a light that is wings and canopy coupled with fire/ I can't transcribe their song/ you'd have to be/ there to understand/ the end of the line/ where nothing cries/ no want because/ no birth/ just life/ a livid red wire/ electric moon radio waves/ blackouts erased/ I hear knocking at the door/ and ignore it/ I hear you yelling on the street/ you may not come in/ I keep walking up the stairs/ one by one I rise/ as your voices grow far and faint/ the hot lamp/ flickers flat doubles/ of my face against/ an endless wall/ papered with the watching dead

Suspiria

The rain's a dance/ rehearsal/ that never ends/ sheet after sheet after sheet/ draped and gauzy/ bloodied glass arabesques/ beyond light/ I turned my head/ and there was a witch/ in cypress needles/ knobbed and knuckled I wanted/ to get closer/ but can't reach/ her cold tongue/ no matter how close/ she passes/ but I touch/ and am revolted/ riveted/ riven/ with thick pigment/ and think of mold/ a growing green skin/ over forgotten milk/ cupped inside my breast/ of course/ men invented time/ to cross-stitch the costumes/ on tighter than blood/ and leaves are their own/ hour hands/ clocks chased/ with feverwater and/ finger-painted irises around a window/ blinking red sun/ between lamps in the courtyard/ below a room of sharp-boned/ women working hard/ at pointing their toes/ to a metronome's swing/ rip rip/ blades through a rib/ cage bird feathers/ everywhere glued to the ceiling/ with sticky saffron paint/ I've never been more scared of anything/ than I am of myself/ as I leave/ the forest for the city/ happy to be/ sad in both/ truth be told/ there was a mosaic/ outside a dance academy/ in New Orleans where I stood/ staring through myself/ goblinesque in mirror shards pressed/ against angry clay/ barbed voices in the night/ an ugly bathroom vanity/ its smashed particulars set/ to look like razor flames/ crowning a stabbed heart/ yes it was dramatic/ as all that/ I raised my voice/ high and it crashed/ candied alive/ hidden with keening cats/ in tall grass

House

We/ girls get together/ after the bomb/ we girls/ aglow in aftermath/ an angry cat/ we get on each other's/ nerves/ exposed piano wires/ we flood our own/ homes with the how/ and the much/ of our growing/ our sorrow baths/ the night I drank/ a bottle of orange/ wine on beige/ carpet I was swimming/ farther away/ from the girls/ I was/ wasn't I/ listening/ I could still hear/ myself laugh/ like eyes open bright/ looking out from an onyx/ well/ under reddened night/ girls delight in shipwreck/ when we describe an explosion/ it is always as something/ else/ mushrooms grown from corpse pots/ in a window box/ look/ lightning striking waves/ I lived in the room/ with a sinking piano/ everyone out there/ was getting sick/ coughing/ or just thinking/ about coughing/ the worst disease/ is one that mimics a mind/ streaming red dye/ it is dangerous/ to breathe/ and go on/ girls on the floor/ flipping glossy pages/ girls casting love spells/ I let my cheek settle/ onto the carpet/ pinkly/ a shell/ how Venus formed/ from foam and viscera/ girls/ our beauty is a monster

Vertigo

Certainly it has to be/ me hanging in the gallery/ and on the bench/ watching myself sit/ for the portrait/ I am/ the woman/ but am I/ the woman watching me/ watch myself through the hard/ dark resin reddened by centuries of sun/ a portrait of an unidentified lady/ varnished nameless in lace/ amber shellac shadows my cheek and dress/ all those bouquet days/ I slumped hungover at the Met/ here to remember all/ the different gazes of death/ inside life and after/ room to room/ women's mouths and noses and eyes and fingers/ spin a hole in my chest/ my shoes shuffle along the smooth corridor/ causing sparks to stab my legs where/ my seafoam dress swings/ one leg slightly bigger/ than the weaker other/ it's the smallest things/ that make me want to be/ somebody else/ every minute I'm breathing/ in circles spiraling/ the veined marble stairs through clean glass/ doors past Titian's chubby cupids/ chasing after me/ and who then will my blood/ flow through next I ask the angels/ as they crawl up and down/ the eggshell walls/ a great height shakes/ when I see my feet/ robins quiver/ out the window behind our shoulders/ all of us full/ of pomegranate seeds/ we unknown women/ never do die/ my pulse swelters/ a swollen peach in Dutch/ light/ a life well split/ segmented and captured/ covered in delicately rendered/ ebony flies

~

The worm moves on,
leaves you plump
with furrowed dirt. A
mother's hooded urn.

Standing in the rain
you grow new entrails
from shed petals,
pinecones, and hair,
wasp stingers and sap
scum.

A phantom coil
swells your limbs.

Your trunk riveted
with new needles and
knots.

*Tell me, at least, I tasted
good.*

With one hand, you
reach for a bag of sea
salt and soot and the
other grabs its last
ring

pulling, pulling—
one half-severed—

the other seared—

Rosemary's Baby

All mothers make monsters/ cradle what seeps through black crepe/ I have my father's eyes/ which were his mother's/ and hers before/ a sharpened line of looking/ hard at the sky/ to notice where the smoke is blowing/ and which clouds/ most resemble/ claws/ scratched down the earth's back/ the fiery exhaustion/ of flown expectations/ a green scarf around my wet hair/ I watch crowds part/ on Madison Avenue/ in December/ see how everyone moves/ molecular tricks over glass/ windows dressed with festive/ sylphs/ draped for ritual/ exchanges of gold/ tomorrow's costume/ this is my year/ things are looking/ up at the highest towers/ as I recite my lines to traffic lights/ my teeth like white paint/ spilled across macadam/ smiles raw as steam/ I call myself/ a woman/ on her way home/ hiding in the phonebooth/ at a loss for/ words even when/ opening the door/ I am always a new/ beginning a being/ that ends every/ second with a feral thump/ in my chest/ open the pouch full/ of letters spelling/ a spell cast under still sun/ its spangled jaws broke/ the first word/ yes I want so badly/ to feed my demons/ let the monsters/ inside myself/ grow

Hereditary

First/ a wail and/ I knew I/ had been born/
when a frozen sea appeared/ at the cradle/
crammed with everything I can't know/ or
understand/ my room painted/ aqueous
blue/ and a whale's slow shadow swam over
the ceiling/ when nothing came/ to light / I
gave birth to a sea cow/ wore inky wool/ and
scratched a hole/ in the center/ of my chest
where I/ a growling child sat/ drawing eels/
curling shipwrecks around/ my cold wet ear

Picnic at Hanging Rock

A hot day/ to hang your head/ let it go gooey/ red jelly candies in the sun/ pink bodies drooped over stone/ and the minute the universe breaks/ old lava and magma makes/ the earth form over/ again with scalded waves/ inside our locked girlish chests/ wanting what comes/ from a sky without moons/ and broken bones/ to let us rest/ with the last words in a book bent/ over our eyes for shade/ unsheltered and vaporous where it hangs/ half remembered/ as lessons erased from a wet page/ waking to a silver scoop/ in melon flesh the funny way/ cantaloupe sounds when cut out/ cold orange bulbs eloping/ with the tongue/ planetary they spin and sink/ in an ocean the first/ notion of fingertips dipped below/ orbs with runny yolks/ our eggs look so like promises/ how tomorrow might be/ had the ground not/ asked us back/ had the air not pulled us/ apart and made heat/ rise through canyons/ our limbs climbing inside/ where did we go where/ did we go/ bright and vanished/ doesn't death feel warm/ to the touch/ sandstone hands/ open/ empty nebulae but/ a hard human/ kind

Camp Crystal Lake

Slate slaps my face/ first as wave/ and then as a lucky/ rock skipped by a boy/ on shore/ an ancient thing/ to be hit/ and not see it coming/ a gray chill/ one splits the other/ swallows my smaller/ body wanting to wash/ away flesh and render/ me agate/ sentient sediment/ I have nothing/ to say because/ in pain/ words implode on the spot/ I'm struck/ language with nowhere to escape/ makes a bruised temple/ of ancestral chanting I/ wade to the pebbled/ beach on my knees/ forehead pressed against cold worry/ stones and the boys/ are gone/ their laughter laps/ at my feet/ granite clouds/ on skull

~

Unworried, the worm
has survived worse. It
inches   infinitely
ingesting   gashes
stuffed   with   apple
skins,   bone   meal,
shells,   horn   dust,
dried   starfish   and
wool waste.

The   worm   retreats
grave-deep   into   cold
black dirt. Halved and
halved   and   halved
into undead selves.

Nightcrawlers   .
begetting succulence
and ash.

The   worm   worms
around—longing   for
a hook, a fish, a queen
to feed.

In its wake your body
is a sapling sprouting
vines   of   beating
hearts through open
pores—

your   new   mouth,   a
nest   of   snake   eggs,
beehives   for
fingertips. A husk in
bloom.

The Brood

[go on] [wait but be born] [be born] [en masse

be] [born in symphonic] [amniotic aftershocks]

[a burst a bludgeon] [a bloom as soon] [as it

erupts] [and wait and] [wait] [and wait I didn't]

[mean to] [have so many] [hungry larvae] [starve

under my folds] [none took] [hook to soil] [green

sounded like night] [and night was soaking] [with

ribald aphids] [the rhythmic stutter] [whole

colonies grinding] [leaves with yellow] [legs and

then] [the thick knitted] [drone clawing out]

[from under] [every wing] [says let me back] [in]

DIY Bingo for the Living and the Dead

	Rise— Rise— Rise—	

Note Stitched Across the Monster's Wrists

My creator - - - the sun - - - hid itself behind - - - another world - - - dressed in - - - a thin - - - black -

- - veil - - - I bore - - - the gentle words - - - hideously deformed - - - by the throats - - - of little winged

- - - animals - - - I looked - - - into the live embers - - - thrust my hand - - - among daemons of hell -

- - a paradise - - - and dank earth - - - stones and wood - - - I saw none - - - like me- - - - - - - - - - - -

All Tomorrow's Parties

A dialogue/ between thrumming pines/ scrawled in whiteout on a whiteboard/ when you're walking directly into a headwind/ you stop existing/ in a stable sense/ everything is always spinning/ even the dead do/ I walk into a party in a too-small room/ in the basement of a burning archives/ plates of garlands and papaya flesh/ the place crowded with scribes and candelabra/ everyone inventing a language/ on the spot/ I trip to the center of that room/ ankles bleeding/ dragging a trunk of cotton balls and dead moths/ everything spills wall to wall/ and the flow of breath from every mouth blows/ wings and stuffing/ back out until all the words are frail/ painted bodies falling apart/ to the music of flames and crushed buttresses above/ I forget how to introduce myself/ my name is broken pillow/ my name is inferno/ my name is *Acherontia Atropos*/ that is/ death's-head hawkmoth/ I enter rooms swinging the wrong sledgehammers/ still hungry enough/ to stuff my teeth with no birds singing/ living is just a lot/ so I go/ goodbyeless/ through the haze

Python a l'Orange

It was my understanding the fox had buried herself/ for the night/ her scent/ a winding trail/ above the trail itself/ and the hounds had surrendered to the hall/ half asleep with worry/ their muzzles drenched in lemon zest/ the ladies dismounted without complaint/ but the gentlemen lingered/ wondering whether they had any meat left in their skulls/ any hearts to emblazon later upon their chests/ good thing the heat gave way to showers/ good thing the almighty ruin of ignored truths fledged/ the scene as serpents fomenting orange warnings/ from beneath the patio/ put yourself in a quiet mood/ hum a tune reminiscent of pythons boiling/ it's not too late to do something with the rattle

Hush

Suckled blanket nubs—rubber nipple
chandelier—August icing factory
implosion—wet paper cranes—
hummingbird spy craft—clandestine
banana chewing under a laboratory desk
at noon—when the witch stops
burning—ziplocked stash of ordinary
blue rooibos—anything red in a
swimming pool—the tide as
remembered under the influence of
horse tranquilizers—a ghost in stone—
archival light on acid free paper—
heirloom eggshell shoebox—father's
brain fog—news blizzard—you go cool

The American Way of Death II

What happens at the mall/ does not stay/ at the mall/ it is a vapor let loose/ over the outlet/ a buzzed light glitzing antiseptically above/ the valley/ of the shadow/ of/ commerce/ causing many eyelids to twitch/ in unison/ the air goes/ Avon slick/ skin-so-soft/ I am lost/ to possibilities/ and the denim conundrums/ of my youth/ a soft pretzel/ motif/ my mother/ can't find me/ so has my name/ announced on the intercom/ and I die/ right there/ from desire for/ a new name/ splashing backwards into the wishing pool/ thousands of/ coins pour out of my mouth/ enough to buy/ a black wax parking lot/ scented candle/ that/ when lit/ produces a sizzle/ of shredded red t-shirts/ wet shoelaces stuck in an escalator/ going up/ up/ heavenward/ into atrium glass/ then sky/ into afternoon clouds/ beyond clearance sales/ blasting through/ all wishes hardened/ into expectation/ a zirconia thunderclap/ on the back/ pennies pelting into an empty jar/ save up/ for your funeral pyre/ today is busy/ highlighting her hair/ to look young/ again/ you/ girl/ wandering through aisles of vividly realized/ plastic horses/ they might start galloping/ I hear/ heavy breathing/ my name/ echoed/ please come to the information desk/ your mother is waiting/ for you/ waiting for you/ here

Dark Archive Bingo

Sinking rafts of rag paper bundles—	A gutter where ribbon binds papers so long, untied is branded, aglow—	His poisoned mistress gets at the blankness of what's missing—
Rusted straight pins fasten a soldier's execution papers to his child's lips—	Oceanic parchment trenches where shipwrecks gather—	Final asylum is a drawer full of passport photos with enough eyes to see the future—
Look into the kid skin, disputes shredded & akin to sea grass at high tide—	Bloody hinge—	Hushed & impossible to read in this light—
Bound in corners on wet cellar floors, wars, disasters, frost, fires—	Blooming mold creeps black across the bride's lace glove pressed between the pages of her daybook—	A moth-eaten account of survival written on silk & held to the window—
Vinegar reek of an undersea adventure film spooled in humid tin cans—	See how you burn yourself alive from within—	This hissing—

Note Stitched Inside the Monster's Ear

I felt - - - light pressed upon - - - the fire -
- - dark and opaque bodies - - - I slaked
my - - - sleep - - I knew - -- rage - - would
tear me to pieces - - alone - - and wept - -

Wuthering Heights, Volume II

                              I could not bear

his hand in her hair

                              ready to tear
        her arm
               her eyes

                                        her ears

                              love will make

        her tongue
               home to

                                             —chains

her eyes

murder you

a word

could break—chains

a syllable
again

she is a bonny beast

that quiet state

                                             breaking bounds

herself and beasts   ˋ

                    slung

                              gauze

          fond of

a hazel switch

quivering

jaws   chewing

                              bits o'

          my garden

my bite

cut

the coal-hole

that's witched

my heart

and made

currant trees

a dangerous

drunk

tongue.

We wanted to plant some flowers there.

the worms writhe

                          I yearn to crush out their entrails!

I vanished

through

                                            glass   slates   storms

            the moor
            creeping up

I   watched the moths

listened to the soft

                                        unquiet

                                        quiet earth.

The Three Beating Hearts of a Headless Queen

Speaking   animal—I   am   a   being—a
buzzing   thing—a   crying   camera—
from   now   on   to   zero—shaken   paper
hive   of   fleeing   bees—this   mind—a

hypothesis   for   meadows—a   glowing—
open   field   lacks   nothing—not   a
reason—not   luxury—not   emptiness—
or   dew—so   do   not   be   numb—to   the

absurd   joy—of   dark   cold   water—
stinging   your   eyes—as   the   kingdom
burns—an   exiled   queen—covered   in
honey—sticks—brightly   to   the   page—

Note Stitched Beneath the Monster's Ribs

-- you   must
create --

.

Notes & Acknowledgements

Thank you to the editors of the following publications in which (at times vastly altered) versions of individual pieces in the book first appeared: *Action, Spectacle; Bear Review; Cul de Sac of Blood; DIAGRAM; Dream Pop; Fence; Ghost Proposal; Harp & Altar; Paperbag; Sixth Finch; South Dakota Review; Tupelo Quarterly; Volt*

~

Much of this book is in conversation with a variety of films, artworks, and books, many of which are based on previous tellings and texts, including:

All Tomorrow's Parties (The Velvet Underground and Nico, 1966), The Brood (Dir. David Cronenberg, 1979), Carnival of Souls (Dir. Herk Harvey, 1962), Carrie (Film adaptation by Brian de Palma, 1976 of Steven King's book, 1974), Friday the 13th (Dir. Sean S. Cunningham, 1980), Gaslight (Dir. George Cukor, 1944), Hereditary (Dir. Ari Aster, 2018), House (Dir. Nobuhiko Obayashi, 1977), Kwaidan (Dir. Masaki Kobayashi, 1964), Leave Her to Heaven (Dir. John M. Stahl, 1945), Picnic at Hanging Rock (Dir. Peter Weir, 1975), Prom Night (Dir. Paul Lynch, 1980), Psycho (Dir. Alfred Hitchcock, 1960), Rosemary's Baby (Dir. Roman Polanski, 1968), Suspiria (Dir. Dario Argento, 1977), The Alphabet (Dir. David Lynch, 1968), The American Way of Death (by Jessica Mitford, 1963), The Bride Stripped Bare by Her Bachelors (artwork by Marcel Duchamp, 1915-1923), The Haunting of Hill House (Shirley Jackson, 1959) and The Haunting (film adaptation by Dir. Robert Wise, 1963), The Heiress (Dir. William Wyler, 1949), Vertigo (Dir. Alfred Hitchcock, 1958)

"Wuthering Heights, Volume I" and "Wuthering Heights, Volume II" are erasures of Emily Brontë's *Wuthering Heights* (1847)

"Note Stitched Across the Monster's Lips," "Note Stitched Above the Monster's Eye," "Notes Stitched Inside the Monster's Mouth," "Note Stitched Across the Monster's Cheek," "Note Stitched Across the Monster's Wrists," and "Note Stitched Beneath the Monster's Ribs" are centos constructed from fragments of Mary Shelley's *Frankenstein* (1818)

~

Extra special thanks to the following people whose practices, knowledge, and generous insights contributed to the formation of this book and provided an abundant sense of community during these strange times, especially: Geoffrey Nutter and friends in the Wallson Glass writing groups; my Tang Gang: Susan Berger-Jones and Wendy Blake; Elaina Ellis, a trusted reader, indeed; Candace Jensen and Bianca Stone; Jac Jemc; Maud Newton; Ariana Reines and The Invisible College. I am also grateful to Mary Ann O'Gorman for her hospitality and providing a space for me to write at the Twisted Run Retreat in Vancleave, MS.

Enormous gratitude to my friends Daisy Abreu, Cynthia Arrieu-King and the caregiver support group, Tess Bradley, Siobhan Ciminera, Agnieszka Czeblakow, Lindsey Ehrenwerth Herman, Elizabeth England, Amber Heaton, Hayley Heaton, Jaimie Kroot, Peter Mandradjieff, Michelle Naka-Pierce, David Sewell, Brad Soucy, Melissa Tedone, Amish Trivedi, and Courtney Weingarten, for walks, talks, texts, memes, Zooms, good times, kindness, and care.

Huge thanks to Traci Brimhall for selecting the chapbook version of this book as winner of the 2023 Snowbound Chapbook Prize; and to Jeffrey Levine and Kristina Marie Darling, thank you for supporting my writing and giving it a home.

With great love to my parents, family, ancestors, and friends.